199 favorite
Bible verses for
TEENS

christian
art gifts®

Contents

You Are ...

#1

Accepted: It's in Christ that we find out who we are and what we are living for.

EPHESIANS 1:11 THE MESSAGE

#2

A new creation: Anyone who belongs to Christ has become a new creation. The old life has gone; a new life has begun!

2 CORINTHIANS 5:17 NLT

#3

Blessed: The LORD bless you and keep you; the LORD make His face shine upon you and be gracious to you; the LORD turn His face toward you and give you peace.

NUMBERS 6:24

#4

Cherished: God pays even greater attention to you, down to the last detail – even numbering the hairs on your head!

LUKE 12:7 THE MESSAGE

#5

Chosen: You are a chosen people. You are royal priests, a holy nation, God's very own possession. He called you out of the darkness into His wonderful light.

1 Peter 2:9 nlt

#6

Designed by God: Body and soul, I am marvelously made! You know me inside and out, You know every bone in my body; You know exactly how I was made, bit by bit, how I was sculpted from nothing into something.

Psalm 139:14-15 The Message

#7

Favored: God raised us up with Christ and seated us with Him in the heavenly realms in Christ Jesus.

Ephesians 2:6

#8

Forgiven: God forgave all our sins. He canceled the record of the charges against us and took it away by nailing it to the cross.

Colossians 2:13-14 nlt

#9

Loved: I am absolutely convinced that nothing – absolutely nothing can get between us and God's love because of the way that Jesus our Master has embraced us.

ROMANS 8:38-39 THE MESSAGE

#10

Saved: From the beginning God chose you to be saved.

2 THESSALONIANS 2:13

#11

Unique: He has made everything beautiful in its time.

ECCLESIASTES 3:11

#12

Victorious: But thanks be to God! He gives us the victory through our Lord Jesus Christ.

1 CORINTHIANS 15:57

Family

Honesty

telling
the truth

Honesty is the first chapter in the book of wisdom.

Thomas Jefferson

#13

I know, my God, that You examine our hearts and rejoice when You find integrity there.

1 Chronicles 29:17 nlt

#14

Be careful to do what is right in the eyes of everybody.

Romans 12:17

#15

An honest answer is like a warm hug.

Proverbs 24:26 The Message

#16

Light is shed upon the righteous and joy on the upright in heart. Rejoice in the Lord, you who are righteous, and praise His holy name.

Psalm 97:11-12

#17

If you embrace the way God does things, there are wonderful payoffs.

ROMANS 2:10 THE MESSAGE

#18

The LORD will withhold no good thing from those who do what is right.

PSALM 84:11 NLT

#19

Honesty lives confident and carefree, but Shifty is sure to be exposed.

PROVERBS 10:9 THE MESSAGE

A **half** truth is

a **whole** lie.

Yiddish Proverb

Kindness

what would Jesus do?

How **beautiful** a **day** can be when **kindness** touches it.

George Elliston

#20

The fruit of the Spirit is love, joy, peace, patience, kindness, goodness, faithfulness, gentleness and self-control.

GALATIANS 5:22-23

#21

No retaliation. No sharp-tongued sarcasm. Instead, bless – that's your job, to bless. You'll be a blessing and also get a blessing.

1 PETER 3:9 THE MESSAGE

#22

Make sure that nobody pays back wrong for wrong, but always try to be kind to each other.

1 THESSALONIANS 5:15

#23

"So whatever you wish that others would do to you, do also to them."

MATTHEW 7:12 ESV

#24

Be kind and compassionate to one another.

EPHESIANS 4:32

Love Makes
the World
Go Round

The sun can break
through the darkest cloud;
love can brighten
the gloomiest day.

William Arthur Ward

#25

Observe how Christ loved us. His love was not cautious but extravagant. He didn't love in order to get something from us but to give everything of Himself to us. Love like that.

EPHESIANS 5:2 THE MESSAGE

#26

Love one another deeply, from the heart.

1 PETER 1:22

#27

Love always looks for the best, never looks back, but keeps going to the end.

1 CORINTHIANS 13:7 THE MESSAGE

#28

These three remain: faith, hope and love. But the greatest of these is love.

1 CORINTHIANS 13:13

#29

Do everything in love.

1 CORINTHIANS 16:14

#30

Don't just pretend to love others.
Really love them.

ROMANS 12:9 NLT

#31

"Love your neighbor as yourself."

MATTHEW 19:19 NKJV

Love is a fruit in
season at all times,
and within the reach
of every hand.

Mother Teresa

Patience

count to 10 ... slowly

Be **patient** enough
to live one day at a
time as **Jesus** taught us,
letting yesterday **go**
and leaving tomorrow
till it **arrives**.

John F. Newton

#32

Now may the Lord direct your hearts into the love of God and into the patience of Christ.

2 THESSALONIANS 3:5 NKJV

#33

The Holy Spirit produces this kind of fruit in our lives ... patience.

GALATIANS 5:22 NLT

#34

As God's chosen people, holy and dearly loved, clothe yourselves with compassion, kindness, humility, gentleness and patience.

COLOSSIANS 3:12

#35

The longer we wait, the more joyful our expectancy.

ROMANS 8:25 THE MESSAGE

#36

Love is patient.

1 Corinthians 13:4

#37

Be patient in trouble, and keep on praying.

Romans 12:12 nlt

#38

The end of a matter is better than its beginning, and patience is better than pride.

Ecclesiastes 7:8

Patience with others is Love.

Patience with self is Hope.

Patience with God is Faith.

Adel Bestavros

R.E.S.P.E.C.T

Respect for ourselves
guides our morals,
respect for others
guides our manners.

Laurence Sterne

#39

Love each other with genuine affection, and take delight in honoring each other.

ROMANS 12:10 NLT

#40

Make the Master proud of you by being good citizens. Treat everyone you meet with dignity.

1 PETER 2:17 THE MESSAGE

#41

Respect those who work hard among you.

1 THESSALONIANS 5:12

#42

Do nothing from rivalry or conceit, but in humility count others more significant than yourselves.

PHILIPPIANS 2:3 ESV

#43

Let love and faithfulness never leave you; bind them around your neck, write them on the tablet of your heart. Then you will win favor and a good name in the sight of God and man.

PROVERBS 3:3-4

#44

Each of you must show great respect for your mother and father.

LEVITICUS 19:3 NLT

#45

"Honor your father and mother."

MATTHEW 19:19

#46

Sensible children bring joy to their father.

PROVERBS 15:20 NLT

Saying "I forgive you."

Forgiveness is the fragrance the violet sheds on the heel that has crushed it.

Mark Twain

#47

"And when you stand praying, if you hold anything against anyone, forgive him, so that your Father in heaven may forgive you your sins."

MARK 11:25

#48

"If you forgive those who sin against you, your heavenly Father will forgive you."

MATTHEW 6:14 NLT

#49

Forgive one another as quickly and thoroughly as God in Christ forgave you.

EPHESIANS 4:32 THE MESSAGE

#50

"I tell you the truth, all sin can be forgiven."

MARK 3:28 NLT

#51

Make allowance for each other's faults, and forgive anyone who offends you. Remember, the Lord forgave you so you must forgive others. Above all, clothe yourselves with love, which binds us all together in perfect harmony.

COLOSSIANS 3:13-14 NLT

Friendship flourishes
at the fountain
of forgiveness.

Wiliam Arthur Ward

Friends

A Definition of Friendship

A **friend** is –

a **push**

  when you've stopped;

a **word**

  when you're lonely;

a **guide**

  when you're searching;

a **smile**

  when you're sad;

a **song**

  when you're glad.

Charlie "T" Jones

#52

A friend is always loyal.

PROVERBS 17:17 NLT

#53

"Love one another the way I loved you. This is the very best way to love. Put your life on the line for your friends."

JOHN 15:13 THE MESSAGE

#54

Two people are better off than one, for they can help each other succeed. If one person falls, the other can reach out and help.

ECCLESIASTES 4:9-10 NLT

#55

"Where two or three are gathered in My name, there am I among them."

MATTHEW 18:20 ESV

#56

Friends come and friends go, but a true friend sticks by you like family.

PROVERBS 18:24 THE MESSAGE

Best
Friends
Forever

A friend hears the song of the heart and sings it when memory fails.

Martin Luther

#57

Laugh with your friends when they're happy; share tears when they're down.

ROMANS 12:15 THE MESSAGE

#58

Kind words are like honey – sweet to the soul and healthy for the body.

PROVERBS 16:24 NLT

#59

The heartfelt counsel of a friend is as sweet as perfume and incense.

PROVERBS 27:9 NLT

#60

Those who refresh others will themselves be refreshed.

PROVERBS 11:25 NLT

#61

Do a favor and win a friend forever; nothing can untie that bond.

PROVERBS 18:19 THE MESSAGE

Conflict

so you've had a fight ...

Argument is the worst sort of conversation.

Jonathan Swift

#62

Dress in the wardrobe God picked
out for you: compassion, kindness,
humility, quiet strength, discipline.
Be even-tempered.

COLOSSIANS 3:12 THE MESSAGE

#63

Sensible people control their temper;
they earn respect by overlooking
wrongs.

PROVERBS 19:11 NLT

#64

"Forgive your friend. Even if its per-
sonal against you and repeated
seven times through the day, and
seven times he says, 'I'm sorry, I
won't do it again,' forgive him."

LUKE 17:3-4 THE MESSAGE

#65

A gentle answer turns away wrath.

PROVERBS 15:1

#66

Hot tempers start fights; a calm,
cool spirit keeps the peace.

PROVERBS 15:18 THE MESSAGE

#67

A friend loves at all times.

PROVERBS 17:17

#68

It is a mark of good character to
avert quarrels.

PROVERBS 20:3 THE MESSAGE

Don't find fault.

Find a remedy.

Henry Ford

 **GoSSip**

"you'll never guess
what I heard ..."

Why do dogs have
so many friends?
Because they wag
their tails and
not their tongues!

Anonymous

#69

Troublemakers start fights; gossips break up friendships.

PROVERBS 16:28 THE MESSAGE

#70

Mean people spread mean gossip; their words smart and burn.

PROVERBS 16:27 THE MESSAGE

#71

Do not let any unwholesome talk come out of your mouths, but only what is helpful for building others up according to their needs, that it may benefit those who listen.

EPHESIANS 4:29

#72

A gossip goes around telling secrets, so don't hang around with chatterers.

PROVERBS 20:19 NLT

#73

Listening to gossip is like eating cheap candy; do you want junk like that in your belly?

PROVERBS 26:22 THE MESSAGE

#74

From a wise mind comes wise speech; the words of the wise are persuasive. Kind words are like honey – sweet to the soul and healthy for the body.

PROVERBS 16:23-24 NLT

Whoever gossips

to you will gossip

about you.

Spanish Proverb

The Right Friends

Friends

birds of a feather

A true **friend never** gets in your **way** **unless** you happen to be **going down**.

Arnold H. Glasow

#75

As a face is reflected in water, so the heart reflects the real person.

PROVERBS 27:19 NLT

#76

"Out of the overflow of the heart the mouth speaks. The good man brings good things out of the good stored up in him, and the evil man brings evil things out of the evil stored up in him."

MATTHEW 12:34-35

#77

Young people eventually reveal by their actions if their motives are on the up and up.

PROVERBS 20:11 THE MESSAGE

#78

He who walks with the wise grows wise.

PROVERBS 13:20

#79

Join the company of good men and women, keep your feet on the tried and true paths.

PROVERBS 2:20 THE MESSAGE

#80

As iron sharpens iron, so a friend sharpens a friend.

PROVERBS 27:17 NLT

A true **friend** is someone who **believes** in you –

even when you don't

believe in **yourself**.

Anonymous

Living the Christian Life in a Non-Christian World

What you need to do ...

Believe!

have faith

Faith is the **daring**
of the soul to
go farther than
it can see.

William Newton Clarke

#81

We fix our eyes not on what is seen,
but on what is unseen. For what is
seen is temporary, but what is
unseen is eternal.

2 Corinthians 4:18

#82

Faith is the confidence that what
we hope for will actually happen; it
gives us assurance about things we
cannot see.

Hebrews 11:1 nlt

#83

We walk by faith, not by sight.

2 Corinthians 5:7 esv

#84

"All things are possible to him who
believes."

Mark 9:23 nkjv

#85

Believe in the Lord your God, and
you will be able to stand firm.

2 Chronicles 20:20 nlt

What you need to do ...

 Shine!

be a light for Jesus

All the **darkness** of
the world **cannot**
put out the light of
one small **candle**.

Anonymous

#86

"Let your light so shine before men, that they may see your good works and glorify your Father in heaven."

MATTHEW 5:16 NKJV

#87

The ways of right-living people glow with light; the longer they live, the brighter they shine.

PROVERBS 4:18 THE MESSAGE

#88

You are a chosen people, a royal priesthood, a holy nation, a people belonging to God, that you may declare the praises of Him who called you out of darkness into His wonderful light.

1 PETER 2:9

#89

Light shines on the godly, and joy on those whose hearts are right.

PSALM 97:11 NLT

#90

Don't let anyone look down on you because you are young, but set an example for the believers in speech, in life, in love, in faith and in purity.

1 TIMOTHY 4:12

#91

How can a young person stay pure? By obeying Your word. I have tried hard to find You – don't let me wander from Your commands. I have Your word in my heart, that I might not sin against You. I praise You, O LORD; teach me Your decrees.

PSALM 119:9-12 NLT

Attempt **great** things for **God, expect** great **things** from God.

William Carey

What you need to do ...

 **Smile!**

be joyful

A good laugh is a
mighty good thing.

Herman Melville

#92

My heart rejoices in the LORD; for I
delight in Your deliverance.

1 SAMUEL 2:1

#93

The joy of the LORD is your strength.

NEHEMIAH 8:10 NKJV

#94

This is the day the LORD has made;
let us rejoice and be glad in it.

PSALM 118:24

#95

The LORD is my strength and my
song; He has become my salvation.

PSALM 118:14 ESV

#96

Give thanks in all circumstances, for
this is God's will for you.

1 THESSALONIANS 5:18

#97

I am overwhelmed with joy in the LORD my God!

ISAIAH 61:10 NLT

#98

Our hearts brim with joy since we've taken for our own His holy name.

PSALM 33:21 THE MESSAGE

Smiling is infectious,

You can catch it like

the flu. Someone smiled

at me today, and I

started smiling too.

Anonymous

What you need to do ...

 **Speak!**

tell others about Jesus

We share our faith
because of the love
of God that is shed
abroad in our hearts.

David Harvard

#99

God has given us the task of telling everyone what He is doing. We're Christ's representatives.

2 CORINTHIANS 5:19-20 THE MESSAGE

#100

"Go into all the world and proclaim the gospel to the whole creation."

MARK 16:15 ESV

#101

"I tell you the truth, no one can see the kingdom of God unless he is born again."

JOHN 3:3

#102

Those who lead many to righteousness will shine like the stars forever.

DANIEL 12:3 NLT

#103

"You are My witnesses," declares the LORD.

ISAIAH 43:10

Your support system ...

Other
Christians

... for fellowship

The church is the
gathering of God's
children, where they
can be helped and fed
like babies and then,
guided by her motherly care,
grow up to manhood
in maturity of faith.

John Calvin

#104

All of you should be of one mind ...
Love each other.

1 Peter 3:8 NLT

#105

If we are living in the light, as God is
in the light, then we have fellowship
with each other.

1 John 1:7 NLT

#106

Let us not give up meeting together,
as some are in the habit of doing,
but let us encourage one another.

Hebrews 10:25

#107

We are many parts of one body,
and we all belong to each other.

Romans 12:5 NLT

#108

"Where two or three come together
in My name, there am I with them."

Matthew 18:20

Your support system ...

 **Prayer**

your power source

The wings of prayer
carry high and far.

#109

"If you believe, you will receive whatever you ask for in prayer."

MATTHEW 21:22

#110

The eyes of the LORD are on the righteous, and His ears are open to their prayers.

1 PETER 3:12 NKJV

#111

The earnest prayer of a righteous person has great power and produces wonderful results.

JAMES 5:16 NLT

#112

"When you pray, go into your room, close the door and pray to your Father, who is unseen. Then your Father, who sees what is done in secret, will reward you."

MATTHEW 6:6

#113

God's there, listening for all who pray, for all who pray and mean it.

PSALM 145:18 THE MESSAGE

#114

Pray all the time.

1 THESSALONIANS 5:17 THE MESSAGE

#115

Don't quit in hard times; pray all the harder.

ROMANS 12:12 THE MESSAGE

Faith in a prayer-hearing God will make a prayer-loving Christian.

Andrew Murray

Your support system ...

 **The Bible**

your manual

Nobody ever outgrows
Scripture; the book
widens and deepens
with our years.

Charles H. Spurgeon

#116

For the word of the LORD is right and true; He is faithful in all He does.

PSALM 33:4

#117

"Even more blessed are all who hear the word of God and put it into practice."

LUKE 11:28 NLT

#118

God means what He says. What He says goes. His powerful Word is sharp as a surgeon's scalpel, cutting through everything. Nothing and no one is impervious to God's Word. We can't get away from it – no matter what.

HEBREWS 4:12-13 THE MESSAGE

#119

When I discovered Your words, I devoured them. They are my joy and my heart's delight.

JEREMIAH 15:16 NLT

#120

All Scripture is inspired by God and is useful to teach us what is true. It corrects us when we are wrong and teaches us to do what is right.

2 TIMOTHY 3:16 NLT

#121

Your word is a lamp to my feet and a light for my path.

PSALM 119:105

A **knowledge** of the **Bible** is essential to a rich and **meaningful** life.

Billy Graham

Growing Pains

Hopelessness

when you want to give up

There are no hopeless situations; there are only people who have grown hopeless about them.

William Barclay

#122

The LORD is good to those whose hope is in Him, to the one who seeks Him; it is good to wait quietly for the salvation of the LORD.

LAMENTATIONS 3:25-26

#123

Now may the God of hope fill you with all joy and peace in believing, that you may abound in hope by the power of the Holy Spirit.

ROMANS 15:13 NKJV

#124

Those who hope in the LORD will renew their strength. They will soar on wings like eagles; they will run and not grow weary, they will walk and not be faint.

ISAIAH 40:31

#125

Having hope will give you courage. You will be protected and will rest in safety.

JOB 11:18 NLT

#126

For You, O LORD, are my hope, my trust, O LORD, from my youth. My praise is continually of You.

PSALM 71:5-6 ESV

#127

Trust steadily in God,
hope unswervingly,
love extravagantly.

1 CORINTHIANS 13:13 THE MESSAGE

If **you** do not **hope**

you will never

discover what is

beyond your hopes.

Clement of Alexandria

Loneliness

when 1 feels like a lonely number

It is **better** to have
one **true friend** than
all the **acquaintances**
in the world.

#128

Those who know Your name trust in
You, for You, O Lord, do not abandon
those who search for You.

PSALM 9:10 NLT

#129

"I will never leave you nor forsake
you."

HEBREWS 13:5 ESV

#130

Even when I walk through the
darkest valley, I will not be afraid,
for You are close beside me. Your
rod and Your staff protect and
comfort me.

PSALM 23:4 NLT

#131

"I will be with you, day after day
after day, right up to the end of the
age."

MATTHEW 28:20 THE MESSAGE

#132

Turn to me and have mercy, for I
am alone and in deep distress.

PSALM 25:16 NLT

#133

God places the lonely in families.

PSALM 68:6 NLT

#134

Those who plant in tears will harvest
with shouts of joy.

PSALM 126:5 NLT

People are lonely
because they build
walls instead of bridges.

Joseph Fort Newton

Peer
Pressure
saying No

The voice of Christ:
"Write My words in your
heart and meditate on
them earnestly, for in
time of temptation they
will be very necessary."

Thomas à Kempis

#135

Keep your eyes open, hold tight to
your convictions, give it all you've
got, be resolute.

1 CORINTHIANS 16:13 THE MESSAGE

#136

Stand firm and be strong in your
faith.

1 PETER 5:9 NLT

#137

Bless those who persecute you. Pray
that God will bless them.

ROMANS 12:14 NLT

#138

Hate what is wrong. Hold tightly to
what is good.

ROMANS 12:9 NLT

#139

Trouble chases sinners, while blessings reward the righteous.

PROVERBS 13:21 NLT

#140

Don't lose sight of common sense
and discernment. Hang on to them,
for they will refresh your soul.

PROVERBS 3:21-22 NLT

#141

Wise living gets rewarded with
honor; stupid living gets the booby
prize.

PROVERBS 3:35 THE MESSAGE

#142

The LORD approves of those who are
good.

PROVERBS 12:2 NLT

Standing Out

when you feel like
you don't fit in

Be Yourself – Truthfully

Accept Yourself – Gracefully

Value Yourself – Joyfully

Forgive Yourself – Completely

Treat Yourself – Generously

Love Yourself – Wholeheartedly

Trust Yourself – Confidently

Empower Yourself – Prayerfully

Give Yourself – Enthusiastically

Express Yourself – Radiantly

#143

It is the Lord who made us, and we are His; we are His people, the sheep of His pasture.

PSALM 100:3 NLT

#144

We are God's masterpiece. He has created us anew in Christ Jesus.

EPHESIANS 2:10 NLT

#145

I praise You because I am fearfully and wonderfully made; Your works are wonderful.

PSALM 139:14

#146

Unlike the culture round you, always dragging you down to its level of immaturity, God brings the best out of you, develops well-formed maturity in you.

ROMANS 12:2 THE MESSAGE

#147

"My prayer is not for the world, but for those You have given Me, because they belong to You. All who are Mine belong to You, and You have given them to Me, so they bring Me glory."

JOHN 17:9-10 NLT

#148

How great is the love the Father has lavished on us, that we should be called children of God! And that is what we are!

1 JOHN 3:1

God loves each
one of us as if
there were only
one of us to love.

St. Augustine

Stress

take a chill pill

Be absolutely
de**termined** to
enjoy what you do.

Gerry Sikorski

#149

"When you go through deep waters I will be with you. When you go through rivers of difficulty, you will not drown."

ISAIAH 43:2 NLT

#150

You revive my drooping head.

PSALM 23:5 THE MESSAGE

#151

"Be still, and know that I am God."

PSALM 46:10

#152

Be brave. Be strong. Don't give up.

PSALM 31:24 THE MESSAGE

#153

Those who trust in the LORD will find new strength.

ISAIAH 40:31 NLT

#154

"Are you tired? Worn out? Come to Me. Get away with Me and you'll recover your life."

MATTHEW 11:28 THE MESSAGE

#155

Those who look to Him for help will be radiant with joy; no shadow of shame will darken their faces.

PSALM 34:5 NLT

Celebrate life.
Dream, explore, and
find peace in the
adventure of life.

Anonymous

Schoolwork

do your best

If we all **did** the
things we are
capable of doing,
we would literally
astound ourselves.

Thomas Edison

#156

Commit to the LORD whatever you do, and your plans will succeed.

PROVERBS 16:3

#157

I can do everything through Christ, who gives me strength.

PHILIPPIANS 4:13 NLT

#158

Whatever you do, work at it with all your heart, as working for the Lord.

COLOSSIANS 3:23

#159

The LORD blesses you with bountiful harvests and gives you success in all your work.

DEUTERONOMY 16:15 NLT

#160

All hard work brings a profit.

PROVERBS 14:23

#161

Be strong and do not give up, for your work will be rewarded.

2 Chronicles 15:7

#162

"Let your good deeds shine out for all to see, so that everyone will praise your heavenly Father."

Matthew 5:16 nlt

Far and away the best prize that life offers is the chance to work hard at work worth doing.

Theodore Roosevelt

Worry

when troubles weigh
you down

Take plenty of
time to **count**
your **blessings**,
but **never** spend a
minute in **worry**.

Anonymous

#163

The LORD will take delight in you with gladness. With His love, He will calm all your fears.

ZEPHANIAH 3:17 NLT

#164

Trust in the LORD with all your heart and lean not on your own understanding. In all your ways acknowledge Him, and He will make straight your paths.

PROVERBS 3:5-6

#165

The LORD is near to all who call upon Him, to all who call upon Him in truth.

PSALM 145:18 NKJV

#166

Don't get worked up about what may or may not happen tomorrow. God will help you deal with whatever hard things come up when the time comes.

MATTHEW 6:33 THE MESSAGE

#167

The LORD is for me, so I will have no fear. What can mere people do to me?

PSALM 118:6 NLT

#168

Be anxious for nothing, but in everything by prayer and supplication, with thanksgiving, let your requests be made known to God; and the peace of God, which surpasses all understanding, will guard your hearts and minds.

PHILIPPIANS 4:6-7 NKJV

#169

When doubts filled my mind, Your comfort gave me renewed hope and cheer.

PSALM 94:19 NLT

#170

Cast all your anxiety on Him because He cares for you.

1 PETER 5:7

Directions ...

 What Next?

thinking about the future

The future is as
bright as the
promises of God.

Adoniram Judson

#171

The LORD will work out His plans for my life.

PSALM 138:8 NLT

#172

"For I know the plans I have for you," declares the LORD, "plans to prosper you and not to harm you, plans to give you hope and a future."

JEREMIAH 29:11

#173

The eyes of all look to You in hope; You give them their food as they need it. When You open Your hand, You satisfy the hunger and thirst of every living thing.

PSALM 145:15-16 NLT

#174

There is surely a future hope for you, and your hope will not be cut off.

PROVERBS 23:18

#175

Let all that I am wait quietly before God, for my hope is in Him.

PSALM 62:5 NLT

#176

We know that for those who love God all things work together for good, for those who are called according to His purpose.

ROMANS 8:28 ESV

#177

"Do not be afraid or discouraged. For the LORD your God is with you wherever you go."

JOSHUA 1:9 NLT

The *future* belongs to those who *believe* in the *beauty* of their *dreams*.

Eleanor Roosevelt

Directions ...

Which Way?

directions for the
road map of life

Where God guides,
He provides.

#178

Show me the right path, O LORD;
point out the road for me to follow.

PSALM 25:4 NLT

#179

Your word is a lamp to guide my
feet and a light for my path.

PSALM 119:105 NLT

#180

The LORD directs the steps of the
godly. He delights in every detail of
their lives.

PSALM 37:23 NLT

#181

You've got my feet on the life path,
all radiant from the shining of Your
face. Ever since You took my hand,
I'm on the right way.

PSALM 16:11 THE MESSAGE

#182

Trust God from the bottom of your heart; don't try to figure out everything on your own. Listen for God's voice in everything you do, everywhere you go; He's the one who will keep you on track.

PROVERBS 3:5-6 THE MESSAGE

#183

If any of you lacks wisdom, he should ask God, who gives generously to all without finding fault, and it will be given to him.

JAMES 1:5

If we let **Him**, **God** will **show** us where to **place** our **feet**.

Anonymous

Scripture Verses to Have on Speed Dial

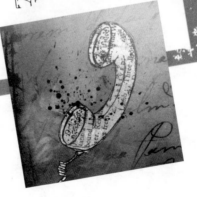

Encouragement

when you feel down

The greatest **oak** was once a little *nut* who **held** its ground.

Anonymous

#184

Blessings crown the head of the righteous.

PROVERBS 10:6

#185

The LORD is good to those who depend on Him, to those who search for Him.

LAMENTATIONS 3:25 NLT

#186

No eye has seen, no ear has heard, no mind has conceived what God has prepared for those who love Him.

1 CORINTHIANS 2:9

#187

My cup brims with blessing. Your beauty and love chase after me every day of my life.

PSALM 23:5-6 THE MESSAGE

#188

The LORD is good. He cares for those who trust in Him.

NAHUM 1:7

#189

May the LORD bless you and protect you. May the LORD smile on you and be gracious to you. May the LORD show you His favor and give you His peace.

NUMBERS 6:24-26 NLT

#190

Delight yourself in the LORD and He will give you the desires of your heart.

PSALM 37:4

#191

Light shines on the godly, and joy on those whose hearts are right.

PSALM 97:11 NLT

# Help

for times when you need
comfort and strength

There can be *no* *rainbow* without a cloud and a **storm** first.

#192

Commit your way to the LORD, trust also in Him, and He shall bring it to pass.

PSALM 37:5 NKJV

#193

I call on You, O God, for You will answer me; give ear to me and hear my prayer.

PSALM 17:6

#194

I know the LORD is always with me. I will not be shaken, for He is right beside me. No wonder my heart is glad, and I rejoice. My body rests in safety.

PSALM 16:8-9 NLT

#195

"I am with you always, to the end of the age."

MATTHEW 28:20 ESV

#196

"Call upon Me in the day of trouble;
I will deliver you."

PSALM 50:15 NKJV

#197

My God will supply every need of
yours according to His riches in glory
in Christ Jesus.

PHILIPPIANS 4:19 ESV

#198

"I am leaving you with a gift – peace
of mind and heart. And the peace I
give is a gift the world cannot give.
So don't be troubled or afraid."

JOHN 14:27 NLT

#199

Trust God from the bottom of your
heart; don't try to figure out everything on your own.

PROVERBS 3:5 THE MESSAGE